RACE

RACE

a play

DAVID MAMET

THEATRE COMMUNICATIONS GROUP
NEW YORK
2010

Race is published by Theatre Communications Group, Inc., 520 Eighth Avenue, 24th Floor, New York, NY 10018-4156

This publication is made possible in part with public funds from the New York State Council on the Arts, a State Agency.

TCG books are exclusively distributed to the book trade by Consortium Book Sales and Distribution.

Library of Congress Cataloging-in-Publication Data

Mamet, David.
Race / David Mamet.—1st ed.
p. cm.
ISBN 978-1-55936-382-2
1. Lawyers—Drama. 2. African American lawyers—Drama. 3. Trials (Rape)—Drama. 4. Race—Drama. 5. Race relations—Drama. I. Title.
PS3563.A4345R33 2010
812'.54—dc22 2010038898

Book design and composition by Lisa Govan
Cover photo by Devon Moore Curtin / Getty Images
Cover design by Serino Coyne

First Edition, November 2010

THIS PLAY IS DEDICATED TO SHELBY STEELE

RACE

PRODUCTION HISTORY

Race premiered on Broadway on December 6, 2009, at the Ethel Barrymore Theatre (Producers: Jeffrey Richards; Jerry Frankel; Jam Theatricals; JK Productions; Peggy Hill and Nicholas Quinn Rosenkranz; Scott M. Delman; Terry Allen Kramer/James L. Nederlander; Swinsky Deitch; Bat-Barry Productions; Ronald Frankel; James Fuld, Jr.; Kathleen K. Johnson; Terry Schnuck; The Weinstein Company; Marc Frankel; Jay and Cindy Gutterman/ Stewart Mercer). The production was directed by David Mamet, with scenic design by Santo Loquasto, costume design by Thomas Broecker and lighting design by Brian MacDevitt; the production stage manager was Matthew Silver. The cast was:

JACK LAWSON	James Spader
HENRY BROWN	David Alan Grier
SUSAN	Kerry Washington
CHARLES STRICKLAND	Richard Thomas

THE SCENE

An office

THE CHARACTERS

JACK LAWSON and CHARLES STRICKLAND	two white men in their forties
HENRY BROWN	a black man in his forties
SUSAN	a black woman in her twenties

SCENE ONE

An office.
Jack, Henry, Charles and Susan onstage.

HENRY: Sit down.

(Charles holds an overcoat, which Susan takes from him. Charles sits.)

You want to tell me about black folks? I'll help you: O.J. Was guilty. Rodney King was in the wrong place, but the police have the right to use force. Malcolm X. Was noble when he renounced violence. Prior to that he was misguided. Dr. King was, of course, a saint. He was killed by a jealous husband, and you had a maid when you were young who was better to you than your mother. She raised you. You've never fucked a black girl, but one sat near you in science class, and she was actually rather *shy*.

(Pause.)

CHARLES: . . . I would never say *any* of . . .

HENRY: You're fucking A right you wouldn't. Which is the purpose of the lesson. Do you know what you can say? To a black man. On the subject of race?

CHARLES: "Nothing."

HENRY: That is correct.

(Pause.)

CHARLES: *Black* people can talk about Race.

HENRY: How about that.

(Pause.)

CHARLES: I will do anything I can. To wipe the slate clean.

JACK: You cannot wipe the slate clean.

HENRY: Mmm-hmm.

JACK: You say it isn't fair? It is neither fair nor unfair. None of us is immune. From a false accusation.

CHARLES: You know it is false?

JACK: I will assume that it is false.

CHARLES: Why?

JACK: Because you will be paying us to support that assumption.

CHARLES: And if I were *not* paying you?

JACK: I would assume that you are guilty.

CHARLES: Why?

JACK: Because it makes a better story.

HENRY: World goes to sleep at night Mr. Strickland. Wakes up and it needs two things. A cup of coffee and some vicious gossip.

CHARLES: And you can change the world.

HENRY: No one can change the world.

CHARLES: But you could perhaps change. The outcome in this instance, of that accusation.

JACK: You would be paying us for our ability. In good faith. To extend all our powers. To attempt to do so.

CHARLES: In a cause in which you did not believe.

JACK: Belief. Cannot be controlled. One believes. People are good, people are bad. God exists. Or the Mob killed Kennedy. The appearance of belief. May be induced or *extorted*. People may be: coerced, seduced or suborned, into momentarily acting against their beliefs.

CHARLES: "Induced or extorted."

HENRY: The Law, Mr. Strickland, is not an exercise in metaphysics. But an alley fight.

JACK: Why are you here?

CHARLES: I want your help.

JACK: "But—?"

CHARLES: But I would like you to *believe* me.

JACK: Why?

CHARLES: Because I feel that would make you more effective advocates.

JACK: Let me enlighten you. "*Belief,*" sir, hamstrings the advocate. Who is, then, "anchored to the facts." I "believe" in the process. Whereby: each side is permitted. To engage an attorney. Does this find the truth? Neither side wants the truth. Each wants to prevail. Does society "deserve" the truth? Alright. Will they get it? Never. Why? As the truth is in doubt even to the litigants. Each of whom will lie first to himself, then to his attorney, and then to the court, to bring about an outcome which he deems just. Which is to say, "victory." You understand? And, on the scaffold, the condemned man having lied to his lawyer, the judge, and himself, will then lie to God. That is the long speech. The short speech is: you came here because you think that we can help you. Perhaps we can. What can *you* do?

CHARLES: Alright.

JACK: Listen to our instructions, *obey* them—and cultivate the appearance of contrition.

CHARLES: I didn't *do* anything.

HENRY: You're *white*.

(Pause.)

CHARLES: Is that a crime?

HENRY: In this instance.

(Pause.)

CHARLES: You're kidding.

HENRY: Sadly I am not.

CHARLES *(To Henry)*: Do *you* care that I'm white?

HENRY: "Do I hate white folks?" Z'at your question? "Do all black people hate whites?" Let me put your mind at rest. You *bet* we do. White folks are "scared"? All to the good. You understand? We're thrilled you're guilty.

CHARLES: I'm guilty.

HENRY: Yes.

CHARLES: Because I'm white.

HENRY: No. Because of the *calendar*. Fifty years ago. You're white? Same case. Same facts. You're innocent. *(Pause)* This is the situation. In which you discover yourself.

CHARLES: I understand. You're testing me. I understand.

HENRY: I'm not "testing" you, sir. I'm telling you the truth. Your people, if they were assured by *God*, that you were innocent, would sell you out.

CHARLES: And the blacks?

HENRY: And, to the African-American community.

CHARLES: Alright.

HENRY: You were found fucking one of our women.

CHARLES: I loved her.

HENRY: Isn't that glorious.

CHARLES: And she loved me.

HENRY: Well, I guess she changed her mind.

(Pause; he picks up a newspaper.)

'Cause it says here she says you raped her.

JACK: Alright. I would say I am Jack Lawson, and this is Henry Brown. But you must know that. Because of our race. But you must pretend you do not. Must you not? Here is my question to you: why?

CHARLES: Why?

JACK: Yes. You know that one of us is black and one's white. Why would you pretend to be ignorant of which of us is which?

CHARLES: It's a convention.

JACK: Bravo. There exist conventions which *may be*: outdated, superfluous, offensive, or indeed immoral. But still remain in force. *(Pause)* Having been accused of having broken with convention, your problem is to win from your fellow citizens a pass. There are two ways to accomplish that. The first is to assert you were somewhere *else*, incompetent, coerced or framed. The second is to challenge the convention. Which do you like?

CHARLES: I don't like either of them.

JACK: That's a good start. Now pick one.

CHARLES: Isn't that your job?

JACK: Well, you tell *me*. We're going to roll the dice. But: *you* guess wrong, or we're incompetent, *you* go to jail. I get paid either way.

CHARLES: Well, that's blunt.

JACK: You wanted to hire your brother-in-law. You had that option . . .

CHARLES: I don't *have* a brother-in-law.

HENRY: You had a brother-in-law by your first marriage.

CHARLES: Good for you.

HENRY: I read the papers.

JACK: Everybody reads the papers. That's your problem.

CHARLES: Why do you address me this way?

JACK: "Rich as you are"?

CHARLES: . . . *al*right . . .

JACK: Why did you come to us?

CHARLES: I . . .

JACK: I assume you chose us because of our Racial Makeup. After you went to Greenstein.

HENRY: Why did you leave Greenstein?

JACK: Now the nickel drops.

CHARLES: Can I rely upon your honesty?

JACK: I don't want you relying on our honesty.

CHARLES: Upon what should I rely?

HENRY: Upon our desire for Fortune and Fame.

JACK: Why did you leave Greenstein?

CHARLES: I didn't like the way. He was handling the case.

JACK: What didn't you like about it?

CHARLES: What difference does it make?

JACK: Somebody who hits his first wife *will* hit his second wife. You know why? He's a wife beater.

CHARLES: I didn't like the way that I was being treated.

JACK: Do you have it in contention to plead guilty?

CHARLES: Absolutely not.

JACK: Then, free of charge? You're going to have to drop the rich bit. *(Pause)* Why should we treat you better?

HENRY: 'Cause we're the underdog, and, you would think, we'd have to eat more of your pomposity, and believe your fake contrition.

CHARLES: Who do you think that you're talking to?

HENRY: I think I'm talking to a rapist and race-criminal. And I think you didn't play straight with Greenstein, and you're going to pull the same trick *here,* and walk out on us when things get rough, and leave *us* looking sweet and silly. And turn to the American Public, a misunderstood man, whose lawyers do not "*like*" him. *I* don't like you . . .

JACK: "At some point . . ."

HENRY: And p.s. I don't like all this bullshit about the world is treating you unfairly, as it *also* treated you unfairly when you were born to wealth, but I don't believe that you complained *then*—so let's get that out upon the table *now*—because as it occurs to *me,* be *assured* it will occur to the *jury.*

CHARLES: I want you to represent me.

JACK: Why?

CHARLES: Because . . .

(Pause.)

JACK: Go on.

CHARLES: Because I think you can win.

JACK: And why would you think that?

HENRY: I don't like it.

CHARLES: Because you've won before.

HENRY: Greenstein's won before.

CHARLES: But he's white.

HENRY: So you *do* understand the nature of the case.

CHARLES: I do.

HENRY: And do you understand that it cannot be won. Other than by dealing with the sordid?

CHARLES: The sordid . . .

JACK: How do you think we've won before?

CHARLES: I . . .

JACK: We have *won*. By being *quick*, and being *brutal*. Being fast and first, and tearing off the fucking Band-Aid.

CHARLES: It's very *important* to me, that, let me put it differently. I, of course . . .

JACK: Mr. Strickland, save it.

CHARLES: Save it . . .

HENRY: The surgeon may have time. To do the operation. He does not have time, to wake the fella up, and explain what he's going to cut.

CHARLES: And, I: am the drugged patient . . .

HENRY: You want me to tell you what you are? White man, rich man? You are so fucked-up out of your mind, you don't know which comes first, Christmas or Lincoln's Birthday. You don't know whether to confess or go out and buy a pistol. Now, tell me, you haven't thought about *both*.

(Pause.)

CHARLES: I am the victim. *(Pause)* Of a false accusation.

HENRY: Which of us is immune?

(Henry passes Charles a notepad.)

JACK: Mr. Strickland. We need you to go in the outer office and write down, in effect, "everything you ever did."

CHARLES: I don't understand.

JACK: Yes, you do.

CHARLES: You want me to write . . . ?

JACK: I want you to write. A catalog of your sins.

CHARLES: And what does that have to do with "the facts of this case"?

JACK: There *are* no "facts of the case." There are two *fictions*. Which the opposing teams each seek to impress upon the jury. That is part of the wisdom you'd be paying us for.

CHARLES: And what is the rest?

HENRY: Wisdom you're paying us for, Mr. Strickland, is that you'd better fight dirtier than the prosecution.

JACK: Why is it; *poor* people don't get dragged up in the press? "Manuel went to the massage parlor . . ." "Motishia cheated on her husband . . ."

CHARLES: Why?

JACK: Because it ain't gossip.

CHARLES: "It . . . ?"

HENRY: The legal process, Charles is only about three things.

CHARLES: What are those three things?

HENRY: Hatred, fear, or envy. And you just hit the trifecta.

CHARLES: How do I win this case?

JACK: At this moment, I'll be goddamned if I know.

CHARLES: Well, that's blunt.

JACK: Charles. Everything. Which you have taken for granted. As your right. Is about to land you in jail. Guilty or not. Do you understand? If we begin, "How dare you suggest that you can destroy me?" then the mob will raise you out.

CHARLES: Why?

JACK: Because it knows your name.

HENRY: He might have to beg . . .

(Charles shakes his head.)

You never begged . . .

JACK: You never begged? You were young, you never begged for pussy? You never begged the officer to let you off the D.U.I.?

HENRY: You ever do that?

CHARLES: I'm innocent.

JACK: Nobody fucking cares. You understand. Nobody cares. The only way out is through, and. To get back into the world one way or the other, you're going to have to be cleansed.

CHARLES: Alright

HENRY: "Alright," meaning what?

CHARLES: If I. Submit myself to you. What can you do for me?

JACK: Tell him.

HENRY: Plead to a lesser charge. Let's see what kind of deal we can strike.

CHARLES: Am I entitled to a defense?

JACK: We just offered you the best one that you're going to get.

CHARLES: Some lawyer will take the case.

JACK: That is correct.

CHARLES: I want you to defend me.

JACK: Why?

CHARLES: Because I want to fight.

JACK: Take the pad, and write down. Everything you've ever done.

(Pause.)

CHARLES: Alright. I understand. *(He takes the pad)*

(Susan picks up Charles's overcoat, and escorts him from the room.)

JACK: We have to assume that he offered her money. If he offered her money why didn't she go away? *(Pause)* What does she want?

HENRY: What does she want?

JACK: "Revenge?"

HENRY: In which case . . . *(Susan reenters)*

JACK *(To Susan)*: He just "walked in."

SUSAN: That is correct. He just walked in.

(Pause.)

JACK: What did he say when he walked in?

SUSAN: He told me his name and he said "perhaps you've heard of me."

HENRY: Why'd he leave Nicky Greenstein?

JACK: You want to call him or shall I?

HENRY: I'll call him.

(Henry picks up the phone and dials.)

JACK: He bring anything in with him . . . a *file* . . . ?

SUSAN *(Shakes head)*: He told me his name and asked if he could *speak* to you.

JACK: To me? He asked to speak to me? Uh-huh.

HENRY *(To phone)*: This is Hank Brown. Is he in?

JACK *(To Susan)*: Call Kelley. I need: a copy of the indictment.

SUSAN: Kelley?

JACK: And: the arrest report, write it down, *and* of the testimony of: the First Responding Officers.

SUSAN: That won't be avail . . .

JACK: Just make the call.

HENRY: Robert Kelley.

JACK: . . . and the chambermaid.

HENRY: And of the chambermaid.

SUSAN: How would I . . . ?

HENRY: Kelley will get it.

JACK: I need it now. *(She starts to exit. To Susan)* Keep him busy. He runs out of things to write, chat him up. Make him ask you a question. Get him to, I don't know, fill out a "client *information* form" . . .

SUSAN: Is there such a . . . ?

JACK: Just keep him out there.

HENRY *(To phone)*: Have him call me, will you please. Lawson and Brown. He has the number. *(She hangs up)*

JACK: Wait. How does he look to you?

SUSAN: He looked like a guilty man.

JACK: How does a guilty man look?

SUSAN: Furtive. *False*, uh.

JACK: How would a man look, who's been falsely accused?

(Pause.)

SUSAN: Yes. I see.

JACK: Which one is he?

(Pause.)

SUSAN: I . . .

(Pause.)

Why did you send him out there?

JACK: You tell *me*.

SUSAN: To. *(Pause)* To establish *dominance*, to . . .

HENRY: Guess again.

SUSAN: To decide if we should take the case.

JACK: Well, that's right.

SUSAN: Why would we not?

JACK: Get Kelley. I need more information.

SUSAN: Can't we ask the client.

JACK *(Shakes his head)*: No. He's off the charts.

SUSAN: I don't understand.

HENRY: At this point, he is regressed to the savage. He doesn't understand his state. He's never been here before. And he doesn't like it. No one has said "no" to him. For forty years. His answer *now* is to be abject For one moment. Those people before whom he feels he has *abased* himself in that moment, he will, later, turn on.

SUSAN: That's why he left Greenstein.

JACK: We don't know.

SUSAN: *But* . . .

JACK: Alright . . .

SUSAN: He came here *shopping* . . .

JACK: So?

SUSAN: "So shouldn't we bend over backwards?"

JACK: "To?"

SUSAN: To "please" him . . . ?

HENRY: I think that's what *Greenstein* did.

(The phone rings. Jack answers.)

JACK *(To phone)*: Hello. Kelley? We may have a new client. *(Pause)* Red sequined dress. *(Pause)* That's right. *(Pause)* No, he left

Greenstein. *(Pause)* Dunno yet. I need: the arrest report. Notes of the first responding officer. The testimony of . . . whoever you can get to on the hotel staff. Well—when will you be back . . . *(Pause)* Can you blow them off? No, no I need *you* to do it . . . *(Pause; nods)* The chambermaid . . . The report, they file a report, the chambermaid. *(Pause)* Well, where *are* you . . . ? *(Pause)* Well, when does it land? Alright. Soon as you can. *(Hangs up)*

SUSAN: So: do we take the case?

JACK: Well, that's the question.

SUSAN: Why would we not?

JACK: 'Cause Nicky Greenstein is not stupid. He is one smart Jew.

HENRY: He could of bought the girl off, he did not.

SUSAN: Greenstein would have advised him to buy the girl off?

JACK: As he walked in the door.

SUSAN: How do you know he could have bought her off?

HENRY: Because his purse is basically unlimited.

SUSAN: What if she wanted something else?

HENRY: What would that be?

SUSAN: . . . "contrition."

HENRY: How is that usually expressed? . . .

JACK: He could not or would not have bought the girl off. And he wouldn't plead. Which is why Greenstein fired him.

SUSAN: The lawyer fired the client?

JACK: You bet.

SUSAN: How do you know?

JACK: Because he had a *loser.*

HENRY *(On phone)*: Mister Greenstein please. Hank Brown . . . ?

JACK: . . . alright: what do the blacks think?

SUSAN: You think black people are stupid?

JACK: I think *all* people are stupid. I don't think blacks are exempt . . .

HENRY *(To phone)*: Thank you. *(Shakes his head; hangs up)*

JACK: And I think, you get caught and you want a *pass,* confess to something else, embarrassing or criminal.

HENRY: To wit?

JACK: I dunno. He . . . the girl's half his age, he . . . well, he's *fucking* her . . .

HENRY: He's married?

JACK: Well, yes.

SUSAN: Why did Greenstein fire him?

JACK: He's married to another woman, he's fucking the *black* girl . . .

HENRY: Alright, that's the American Way. We *understand* that, but "the white man ripped my dress off," now it's Simon Legree and Topsy.

JACK: Well. Here's two questions. One, what does it cost us if we lose? What is the second one?

SUSAN: What does it cost us if we win?

JACK: Good for you.

(Pause.)

SUSAN: What's his "Racial History?"

(Pause.)

JACK: "Racial History?"

SUSAN: Yes.

JACK: What's the guy's racial history? To the extent we can we're going to make it up 'cause otherwise in this office we, speaking for the group, do not give a fuck.

SUSAN: We don't?

JACK: Here's what it is is, I ran out of whatever it was I need to give a fuck. Other than as it may affect the interests of our client. Which is to say, of my pocketbook. 'Cause. That's what we, I miss my guess, do for a living. I tried being poor. I didn't like it. Did *you* like it? . . .

HENRY: I didn't like it either.

JACK: I gotta talk to Greenstein.

SUSAN: What do you think happened?

JACK: What do I think happened?

SUSAN: In the room.

JACK: In the *hotel* room?

SUSAN: Yeah.

JACK: How would *I* know?

HENRY: What do you think happened?

JACK: I'll tell you what I think. I *think* that *women*. Just like *men*. In the main, being self-interested, will exploit every advantage they may have. Chief among theirs, youth and beauty. Just as will men, who possess the advantages of being old and rich.

SUSAN: And white.

JACK: You bet. *(Picks up newspaper, reads)* "He ripped off my new sequined dress. He threw me down upon the bed. And raped me." *(Picks up another newspaper, reads)* "Room all askew . . ." *This* motherfucker—looks to me like instigating a *race* riot.

HENRY: But *note*: the order. Putting, to her mind, graver offenses first. "He ripped my dress."

SUSAN: She's a poor girl. She *loved* the dress. It meant respectability.

JACK: *Is* she a poor girl? . . .

HENRY: If she's not, she'll look like one the D.A. puts her on the stand . . .

SUSAN: "He ripped off my red dress."

HENRY: . . . he'll put her up there in a fucking *cotton* sack.

JACK: What did *you* make of him?

SUSAN: *I* thought . . .	HENRY: I'll tell you what *I* thought.

SUSAN: No, go ahead.

JACK: No, you. I want to hear what *you* think.

SUSAN: I thought. Here's a fellow, "charismatic," as they say . . .

JACK: . . . charismatic . . .

SUSAN: . . . *part* of his charisma is his reticence.

HENRY: . . . oh my.

SUSAN: Which we may interpret as reserve, or *manners*.

HENRY: Or standoffishness.

JACK: Which is to say "money."

SUSAN: Or, yes, or we might say "intelligence"? Or quote "natural grace," because nobody's going to come out and admit that they're awed by his money.

HENRY: Well, yeah. But that's the problem with the jury.

SUSAN: Which is?

HENRY: Whatever he did, they're going to hate him.

SUSAN: Sure.

HENRY: Sure why? Because he's white?

SUSAN: You bet.

HENRY: Well—that's the face of the case you *can't* change.

JACK: He flirt with you? He flirted with you, didn't he?

SUSAN: Did he flirt with me, I suppose he did.

HENRY: What'd he do?

SUSAN: He, *I* don't know . . .

HENRY: Oh, yes, the little ways "women 'just know' when a man is interested in her . . ."

SUSAN: That's right.

HENRY: And was he interested in you?

SUSAN: He flirted with me.

HENRY: Yes, deniably.

SUSAN: Well, that's the essence of the act.

(Pause.)

JACK: And so your first impression was . . . ?

SUSAN: I disliked him.

HENRY: Why?

SUSAN: He has a wedding ring.

JACK: That make him guilty of rape?

SUSAN: I think he is guilty.

HENRY: You know that he raped the girl?

SUSAN: He *acts* guilty.

JACK: How does a guilty man act?

HENRY *(To Susan)*: Get Kelley's office. Get his guy on the phone, you have the list.

(Susan starts to exit.)

JACK *(To Henry)*: Hold on. *(To Susan)* How does a guilty man act? *(To Henry)* Hank, what's he doing out there? He got his head in his hands or is he puffing up all righteous?

HENRY: Well let's go see.

(Henry exits.)

JACK *(To Susan)*: How does a guilty man act?

SUSAN: In this instance?

JACK: Yes.

SUSAN: Accused of raping a black woman, he encounters a black woman, who *knows* of the accusation. Who is there to *defend* him, and he flirts with her. What is *that*?

JACK: You tell *me*.

SUSAN: A desire for punishment. He wants to be punished.

JACK: Why?

SUSAN: To be readmitted to the group.

JACK: Why has he been expelled?

SUSAN: Because he's guilty.

JACK: Of rape?

SUSAN: Independent of rape.

JACK: What's he guilty of?

SUSAN: *In* effect: the norm which he *has* violated is: he has been caught in the appearance of a Racial Impropriety. Which would force those who would judge him. Into an intolerable position.

JACK: Tell me.

SUSAN: Whites would think to find him innocent is racism. Blacks would think that to do so is treason.

JACK: Do you think he raped her?

SUSAN: Do *you*?

JACK: I want to know what *you* think.

SUSAN: Why? Because I'm black?

JACK: Sure. And, "women," alright, know things no man knows. *You* look at a man, across a room, you know. What his intentions are.

SUSAN: That's right.

JACK: Ah, so I'm smarter than you thought.

SUSAN: You sure?

JACK: I'll prove it to you. Blacks. Know things no white man knows.

SUSAN: Tell me one thing.

JACK: That the whites will screw you. Any chance we get. We cannot help ourselves.

SUSAN: Now tell me why.

JACK: Because we know you hate us.

(Pause.)

SUSAN: How do we get him out of it?
JACK: Is that what we want?

(Pause.)

SUSAN: Yes.
JACK: Are you sure?
SUSAN: Yes.
JACK: And if we lose?
SUSAN: Are you used to losing?
JACK: Very flattering.
SUSAN: Everyone is entitled to a defense.
JACK: Is that so?
SUSAN: I believe it.
JACK *(To self)*: . . . fucking *country* . . . *(To Susan)* Alright. What are the Two Things. I told you. On Day One.
SUSAN: You have to make them like your guy enough to let him off.
JACK: Or?
SUSAN: Make them like *themselves* enough, for making a quote difficult decision.
JACK: What were the words *I* used?
SUSAN: "Give them a hook upon which to hang their bad judgment."
JACK: Tell me one.

(Pause.)

SUSAN: She's a homewrecker. She's: Destroying the Sanctity of the American Home.
JACK: And why do we "like" him.
SUSAN: *That's* why we like him. We get to discover he's the victim. Everyone loves the victim.

JACK: On a secure line?

SUSAN: . . . yes?

JACK: She's *black*. We cannot *put*. Enough White people. On the jury. To find one who is not afraid. Of being thought prejudiced. By letting him off, on your theory.

SUSAN: Because?

JACK: She can't be a homewrecker.

SUSAN: Why not?

JACK: Black people are allowed to commit adultery.

SUSAN: Is that in the Constitution?

JACK: No. It's in the public mind.

SUSAN: Well, *that's* harsh . . .

JACK: . . . you want the truth or a lie?

SUSAN: Then are you saying that we shouldn't take the case?

JACK: Not under that theory.

SUSAN: Under what theory then?

JACK: Alright. *(Pause)* Let's turn it upside down.

SUSAN: Alright.

JACK: Jury comes in. What do they want?

SUSAN: What?

JACK: To struggle bravely against prejudice, and, then, find our client guilty.

SUSAN: Why?

JACK: Because he's sitting in the dock. Why would the state *put* him there if he was innocent? They are participants in what they conceive of as a "*pageant*." They call it "The Pageant of Justice." Here is its plot: We will serve the law by our rapt attention to the forms—and then, as a reward, find the fellow guilty. *Our* job, is to involve them in a different story.

SUSAN: What is the different story?

JACK: I don't *know*. It's . . . it's . . . maybe it's *not* a pageant . . .

SUSAN: What *is* it?

JACK: Maybe it's a war story.

SUSAN: How does it go?

JACK: War story goes like this: you ain't going to believe this, but this is the God's Truth. End of the day, maybe they let your guy go.

SUSAN: Because he's innocent?

JACK: No, because his entertainer—that would be me—put on a better show. *(Pause)* Didn't they tell you that on the Law Review?

SUSAN: I . . .

JACK: The jury has a story. In their head. About what happened in that room. We have to drive that story out of their heads.

SUSAN: How?

JACK: Tell them a better story.

SUSAN: For example?

JACK: For example. What do you recall, about your trip to Venice?

SUSAN: Why Venice?

JACK: Why not? What do people recall? Of their trip to New York? The Statue of Liberty? They knew that before they came. They go to Paris, but they don't recall the Eiffel Tower. They *knew* the Eiffel Tower. They *recall* the little Flower Lady, and her Funny Dog. When they get home, *that's* what they talk about. The conversation they had with their cab driver. And in the jury box, *that's* what they hold to. The Special Thing that they *alone* appreciated. OUR JOB is to create that experience. Which allows them the illusion of autonomy. Do that in courting, the woman expresses her appreciation, lifting up her dress; in law they do so, by letting your client go free.

SUSAN: They express their gratitude.

JACK: Yes.

SUSAN: By "lifting their dress . . ."

(Henry enters.)

HENRY: We gonna take the case? . . .

JACK: How's the client?

HENRY: Holding.

JACK: I need to talk to Greenstein. And I need the information from Bob Kelley.

SUSAN: Yes. Good.

HENRY: His guy's not picking up.

JACK *(To Susan)*: Call his various numbers, get his guy on the phone. *Email* him our list. I need it now.

(She leaves. The phone rings.)

HENRY *(To phone)*: Yes. *(Covers the phone; to Jack)* Nicky Greenstein.

JACK *(To phone)*: *Nicky*. Yeah, blah blah the weather, and blah blah the market. I heard you lost a client. *(Pause)* Because he came over here. *(Pause)* Why did you think that?

HENRY: Because you've got a Black Partner.

(Pause.)

JACK: "Because I've got a Black Partner." Rosy red apple. *(Pause)* *Thank* you. But, I'm not sure yet. Well, we were hoping perhaps *you* could guide us. *(Pause)* I appreciate it. *(Pause)* I appreciate it very much. *(Pause)* Thank you, Nicky . . . *(Pause)* 'F'I could ask you why . . . *(Covers phone)* "Because of new information." *(To phone)* Because of *what* new inf . . . *(Pause; he gestures for a pad and paper. Henry hands it to him. He writes)* What, they "just came *forward*?" Is that a reliable wit . . . the man *and* the woman. *(Pause)* No. *Thank* you, Nicky. *(Pause)* I don't know. Thank you. I'm in your debt. *(He hangs up)* Our *friend*. It is now reported. *Said*. In the hotel: quote, which was just sworn to. By two witnesses, being the couple in the adjoining room, during the altercation: quote: "I'm going to fuck you now, you little nigger bitch." *(Pause)* Quotation ends.

HENRY: Who are the witnesses?

JACK: Husband and wife. Thirty years married. *(Pause)* And the man's a preacher.

HENRY: Black or white?

JACK: White.

(Pause.)

HENRY: And they've sworn to it?

JACK: That's right.

(Pause.)

HENRY: You know any really rich people, Jack?

JACK: Maybe a couple.

HENRY: You ever know one you could trust?

JACK *(To himself)*: Uh-huh.

HENRY: I'm going to tell you what, Jack. He held out on *Nicky*, he'll hold out on *us*. It's a two-way loss. We lose, we *lost*, we get him *off* what does that make us?

JACK: Because it's a black-white case? . . .

HENRY: Well, that's correct. The case is a *loser*, Jacky, let some kid take it, some kid, doesn't *know* better. He puts on a valiant defense. Everybody understands. It doesn't hurt *him*. Case hurts *us*, Jacky. Either way. *(Pause)* I know you're a "war-horse," and all that, you got blood in your nose.

JACK: Very large fee.

HENRY: Amortize it over x years lost clients. *(Pause)* The case stinks.

(Susan reenters with various papers.)

SUSAN: Copies of: the indictment, the report of the first responding officer, room report, report of the chambermaid, report of the floor supervisor . . .

HENRY: We . . .

SUSAN: . . . chambermaid's late, making up the room, the floor supervisor needs to file a report.

(She hands them the reports.)

HENRY: We're going to pass on the case.

(Pause.)

SUSAN: We're passing on the case.

JACK: Call Mr. Strickland in, and . . .

SUSAN: Why are we passing on the case?

HENRY: Because. Given a choice, we are permitted to choose to pass on the case. *(Pause)*

SUSAN: Then I should give him back his check.

JACK: What check?

SUSAN: He wrote us a check.

JACK: "For?"

SUSAN: You asked me, to have him fill out a "client application form," and . . .

HENRY: . . . we asked you to keep him "busy" . . . ?

SUSAN: And, he *asked*, if we also required a *retainer*, and I said . . .

HENRY: And is it in your limited experience that a potential client, a potential client, come in for a consultation, will voluntarily offer money?

SUSAN: I . . .

HENRY: Or is it in your limited experience that, conversely, the client will employ any means of stealth and *delay* to avoid the payment of bills.

JACK: Leave her alone.

HENRY: . . . which falls within the realm of your experience?

JACK: Henry . . .

HENRY: Well, *no*, this is your Honor Student, let's . . .

JACK: It's *alright* . . .

HENRY: She's *your* science project, Jacky, she's not *mine*. And you were going to take the check?

SUSAN: Yes.

HENRY: And had you had it in contention to give him a *receipt*?

SUSAN: Yes. I was writing him a . . .

HENRY *(To Susan)*: What does it mean *contractually*, if you had accepted the check, and you had given him a receipt. Is there a technical term for that?

(Pause.)

SUSAN: It's called a *retainer*.

HENRY: And what is its definition?

JACK: ALRIGHT, Hank.

HENRY: Is it "a legal *contract*?"

JACK: . . . alright . . .

HENRY: Which means we might be obliged to try his case?

SUSAN: He gave a check to Greenstein . . .

HENRY: I'm sure he did *not*.

SUSAN: Why?

HENRY: Because Greenstein's too fucking smart.

SUSAN: I was simply . . .

JACK: No harm done, alright? We leave the check upon the table. *No harm done.* If he's written the check, don't *touch* it. *(Henry shakes his head)* I'll take *care* of it. It's alright, Henry. Jesus Christ . . .

SUSAN *(Pointing at the door)*: Do you want me to . . . ?

JACK: No, I'll do it. Call Kelley's guy. Tell him. We appreciate the documents . . . *(He shows the file of papers)*

SUSAN: I didn't get them from Kelley.

JACK: No, from "Kelley's guy." Tell him we require no further—

SUSAN: I didn't get them from Kelley's guy. He was not responding.

JACK: You didn't get the documents from Kelley's guy?

SUSAN: No.

JACK: Where did you get them from?

SUSAN: From the D.A.

HENRY: You requested the documents from the D.A.

SUSAN: Yes. *(Pause)*

HENRY: Well, then you might as well take his check, because now we're the Attorneys of Record. *(Pause)* What the *fuck* did you think we were *doing* in here? While you were asked, go out there, look pretty, and *stall* the fellow, while we decided . . .

SUSAN: I believed I was doing as instructed . . .

HENRY: While we decided whether or not to take the case.

SUSAN: You instructed me—

HENRY: Did you fucking *go* to Law School?

SUSAN: I beg your pardon, you *told* me, to take him into the . . .

HENRY: And give him a *magazine*. I'm going to tell you what, you went Blind. *You* went fucking blind. You saw, the Rich Man, Billionaire, *flirted* with you.

SUSAN: I *beg* your pardon.

HENRY: . . . that you tried how many Stupid Fucking Errors you could make in a ten-minute interval.

JACK: Henry, she made a mistake . . .

HENRY: What *I* know, that you do *not* know, is why she made it.

JACK: Why did she make it?

HENRY: Because she let her *color* jump on her *intellect*. *(Pause)* And all you had to do is give him a magazine. *(Pause)* Which.

Because of all your "Ivy League" *training* . . . It seems you found *beneath* you.

JACK: Alright, alright . . .

HENRY *(Reads)*: "And now I'm going to fuck you, you little nigger bitch . . ." *(Pause)* And that's our case.

(Henry puts down the pad. Susan picks it up, reads it, and puts it back down. Pause.)

JACK: Will they *swear* to it?

HENRY: Aw, come *on*, Jacky.

JACK: Will he swear to it?

HENRY: White clergyman gets to say "fuck," "nigger" and "bitch," in one sentence.

(Pause.)

JACK: *Well*: . . .

(Pause.)

HENRY: There are some things, One cannot *say*, Jack . . . And our *client* . . .

JACK: He didn't say it, it's just "alleged" . . .

HENRY: That one cannot "allege," as the mob, *fearful of itself*, will as you say, turn on the alleged, and kill him. How do you *defend* this cocksucker? *(Pause)* I need to tell you something.

JACK: She can stay.

(Pause.)

HENRY: I don't *think* so . . .

JACK: She can stay, Henry.

(Pause.)

HENRY: Alright. If we must. If we are, as it seems we are *wedded* to this case. *(Pause)* It has not been unknown. For Advocates.

To stage a less than Spirited Defense. Of those they *clearly found objectionable.* With results acceptable to all but the accused.

JACK: What if he's innocent?

HENRY: Then tell me how we're going to win this case.

(A phone rings. Henry answers it. Into phone:)

Yes. *(Listens)*

JACK *(To Susan)*: Can one win this case?

SUSAN: You said one can win *any* case.

JACK: And the addendum?

SUSAN: "If one only takes on cases one can win." *(Pause)* I'm truly sorry if I did wrong.

JACK: I know you are.

SUSAN: I'm truly sorry.

JACK: It's called a "mistake." *(Reading)* Copy of the indictment. The report of the first responding officer, room report, report of the chambermaid. Report of the floor supervisor . . .

HENRY *(Hangs up the phone)*: Clerk of the court has called. He's listed us as the Attorneys of Record. And we are to appear with Mr. Strickland tomorrow.

JACK: Who's the judge?

HENRY: Before Judge Johnson. To enter a plea.

JACK: That's great.

HENRY: I say we plead him.

JACK: He won't plead.

HENRY: How do you know?

JACK: 'Cause he just *told* us. *(Pause)* Okay. What do you do on Dead Ground?

HENRY: "On Dead Ground, Fight."

(Jack passes one of the newspapers to Susan.)

JACK: Read it. *(She starts to read; pauses)* Just fucking read the thing.

SUSAN *(Reads)*: He threw me down. He ripped off my red sequined dress . . .

JACK *(Referring to another piece of paper)*: What is this?

SUSAN *(Looking at it)*: Hotel. Floor supervisor's report . . .

JACK: Read it.

HENRY *(Reads)*: " . . . the chambermaid Rosa Gonzales . . . Room fourteen twelve . . . disarray, *disarray*, liquor. Spilled . . . cigarette butts . . ." *(Pause. He looks up; Jack looks at Henry)* What? What?

JACK: Where are the sequins? *(Pause)* Floor supervisor's report. Room all torn up, chambermaid's late making it up.

HENRY: Yes?

(Pause.)

JACK: Cigarette butts. Disarray . . . *(Pause)* No mention of the sequins.

HENRY: I don't . . .

JACK *(Of Susan)*: *She* knows. He ripped the dress off, the room would be *covered* in sequins. It *has* to be. *Tell* him. A sequined dress, you *look* at it wrong, they start to fall off. You walk into that room, that would be the first thing you see. *(Pause)* "He threw me down, he ripped my dress off." *(Pause)* It's *impossible* that room would not be covered in sequins. *(Pause)* It's impossible. *(Pause)*

HENRY: So he didn't rape her?

JACK: How do *I* know. But, we've got a *case*. I *like* it. I fucking *like* it.

SUSAN: He called her "you nigger bitch."

JACK: The couple next door *said.*

HENRY: The couple next door heard "you nigger bitch."

SUSAN: . . . can we impeach them?

HENRY: You impeach them and you lose the jury.

JACK: Alright. You want to be bold?

(Pause.)

HENRY: Old married couple, one of them's a preacher, Jack . . .

JACK: You want to be bold?

HENRY: . . . *tell* me.

JACK: How do you draw attention from a shameful act?

HENRY: "By admitting to a more shameful act."

JACK: They didn't hear "you nigger bitch."

HENRY: They'll swear they did.

JACK: Uh-huh.

HENRY: What did they hear?

JACK: They heard "*My* nigger bitch." *(Pause; to Susan)* Anybody ever call you that, while he was fucking you? Crazy with love? *(Pause)* White man, to say that? Admits to *that* in a courtroom, that's so *shameful* every fucking person on the jury will have to believe him. "I'm going to fuck you now my little nigger bitch."

SUSAN: This isn't about sex, it's about Race.

JACK: What's the difference?

SCENE TWO

Henry and Jack in the office. Henry is reading a report.

HENRY: Hotel room: "Condition, as to be expected, lamps broken, linens in disarray, cigarette butts, liquor bottles . . ."

JACK: This is the maid . . .

HENRY: The *floor* manager. . . . her report recapitulates that of the maid, bit better English. No mention in either . . .

JACK: And the crime scene report . . .

HENRY *(Perusing)*: No mention of sequins.

JACK: *No* mention.

HENRY: No.

JACK: First responding officer is told . . . *(Checks notes)* "He ripped off my dress, he threw me on the bed." . . . *he* sees no sequins. Fresh rookie officer. First felony—bending over *backwards*, do it by the book. "Broken lamp, linens on the floor, liquor bottles." No sequins.

HENRY: . . . and we have the "phrase."

JACK: He called her "*my* little nigger."

HENRY: Is that what he said?

JACK: You bet it is and the jury averts its eyes from the whole fucking incident. Tell me the dress again.

HENRY: Again?

JACK: Where is the dress? The lab?

HENRY: The D.A., do you want me to request the dress?

JACK: No. Tell *Kelley*. Get me, *from* the manufacturer. The specs. The dress material, the *thread*, most importantly the thread, the sequins, need *be*, we will reconstruct the dr . . . The entire dress. What size was the dress? *(To Henry)* . . . you give me ONE WOMAN. In that jury box, if he "ripped off that dress," *any* woman. Knows: somebody *sneezes*, those sequins are coming off that dress like rain.

(Susan enters.)

SUSAN: He is waiting outside.

JACK: What size was the dress?

SUSAN: What size?

JACK: Her dress.

SUSAN: About a two.

JACK: "About" a "two."

SUSAN *(Checks notes)*: Dress was a two.

JACK: About *your* size.

SUSAN: Yes.

JACK: I need, the sales receipt. For the dress. *Stating* the size. The sales receipt and match it to the dress—

SUSAN: Why?

JACK: Because they'll say the dress was too fucking big, too fucking small, mis-*tagged*, and thus invalidates our demonstr . . . he's waiting . . . ?

SUSAN: Yes.

JACK: . . . and thus invalidates our demonstration.

SUSAN: What demonstration?

JACK: We're going to stage a *demonstration*.

HENRY: Yes.

JACK: *Same* dress. Exact same dress. Woman of a similar size, *you* could do it. Woman of a similar size puts on the dress. Somebody. Throws you down.

SUSAN: Throws me down?

JACK: Upon a *mattress* . . . put a bed in the court—you put that bed in the court, people are looking away anyway . . . He throws you *down* . . .

SUSAN: The girl still says "he raped me."

JACK: The dress kills 'em on cross.

SUSAN: On cross.

JACK: We let them bring it up. Girl says, "He threw me down and raped me," now we cross- examine. Model, puts on the dress, sequins fly, we move for a directed verdict.

HENRY: Well this is good.

JACK: *You* could put on the dress.

SUSAN: Why? Because I'm black.

(Pause.)

JACK: Well, it has to be a black girl.

SUSAN: Why?

JACK: Why? BECAUSE, in fact, you put a *white* girl in the dress, what does the jury think . . .

HENRY: "They're using a white girl, so we will not remember the victim is black."

JACK: That's correct—the alleged victim, that's right . . .

SUSAN: . . . he's waiting outside . . .

JACK *(To Henry)*: You want to hotwalk him a moment.

HENRY: Explain it to her.

JACK: She understands.

HENRY: Tell her *anyway*.

(Henry exits.)

JACK: We're going to give the jury a gift.

SUSAN: A gift?

JACK: We're going to give them a surprise. But it works *only* as a surprise.

SUSAN: And the surprise is the dress.

JACK: That's right. Sufficient to get *whosoever's* on the jury, to put aside all the nonsense they think they're supposed to think about race. And rule on the facts. Why? *(Pause)* Because the fucking guy's innocent.

SUSAN: "Nonsense about race."

JACK: That's right . . .

SUSAN: Is it nonsense?

JACK: Most of it is. Sure.

SUSAN: Why?

JACK: Because we're herd fuckin' creatures; and we've all got to go home and face the people on the block.

(Pause.)

SUSAN: Do you think black people are stupid?

(Pause.)

JACK: I think black people are fragile.

SUSAN: Are black people different from other people?

JACK: All people are different. Sometimes they conjoin.

SUSAN: They conjoin.

JACK: Yes.

SUSAN: Into.

JACK: A group. A race. A jury, or an audience. *(Pause)* Sometimes they conjoin into a mob.

SUSAN: And you think black people are fragile.

JACK: I know they are.

SUSAN: Why?

JACK: Because you deal with shame.

SUSAN: "Shame"?

JACK: That's correct.

SUSAN: More than other people?

JACK: All people deal with shame or guilt. Jews deal with guilt. Blacks deal with shame. It's two of the wonderful ways we metabolize feelings of inferiority. Our job. Is to get them on the jury to accept our new definition of the Group to which they belong. Not "the whites" or "the blacks." Not "the well-meaning." Or "the people on my block." But the *new* group—which is called "the jury." Another name for which is, The Audience. We're going to put on a show. And when we "amuse" them—they may forget, their individual allegiances and, *for a moment* be conjoined. But for our entertainment to succeed it has to have, surprise. And if a word gets out of the surprise's *nature*, the surprise will fail, and we will lose.

(Henry enters.)

HENRY: Jack . . .

SUSAN: If word got out about our *strategy*, the other side would win.

JACK: They would.

SUSAN: What could they do . . .

HENRY: Uh . . .

JACK: If the case: hangs upon a sequin, all they'd have to do is *secrete* One Sequin, somewhere in the hotel room . . .

HENRY: Jack . . .

JACK: And there goes our case.

SUSAN: . . . would they do that? . . .

JACK: Oh Yes. So our task is: not to *breathe*, not even to *think* of our little surprise. For, if we can think it, the other side can, too. I would not even tell our *client*. *(To Henry)* What?

HENRY: He wants to go to the press.

JACK: He wants to go to the Press?

HENRY: With this statement.

(He hands the paper to Jack. Jack reads.)

JACK: He wants to give this fucking statement to the *press*.

HENRY: That's right . . .

JACK: Get him in here . . .

(Henry goes out and escorts in Charles.)

Mr. Strickland. It is my assessment. We can win this case.

CHARLES: I'm going to go to the press.

JACK: Mister . . .

CHARLES: Would you read it.

JACK: Mister Strickland, what do you think the press *is*? . . .

CHARLES: Would you read my statement, please?

JACK: The press, Mr. Strickland is the pillory, it is the stocks. It exists to license and gratify envy and greed. It cannot serve you. If you appeal to the press they will tear you apart.

CHARLES: Would you please read my statement.

JACK *(Reads)*: "I believe I was wrong . . . I believe we are all brothers beneath the skin. And though I did not *legally* assault the . . ." *(To Henry)* What do you think?

HENRY: I don't think we're brothers beneath the skin, over the skin, or in any way *associated* with the skin.

JACK: Neither do I.

(Charles takes the paper and reads.)

CHARLES *(Reading)*: "I believe there has been a *misunderstanding*, that though the actual facts of the case are not as the young woman stated . . . perhaps, *perhaps*, on some "moral" level . . ."

HENRY: He thinks he's wronged a girl who loved him.

JACK: Is that what you think?

CHARLES: I . . .

JACK: How did you *wrong* her?

CHARLES: I . . .

JACK: How did you wrong her?

CHARLES: I believe, she found herself in a difficult position and . . .

JACK: You said you didn't do it.

CHARLES: You said you didn't care.

JACK: But did you do it?

CHARLES: No.

JACK: Then what is it you want to confess? Did you *rape* her?

CHARLES: No.

HENRY: That's all you were charged with Mr. Strickland.

JACK: Had you had sex with her before?

CHARLES: Yes.

JACK: Consensual sex?

CHARLES: Yes.

JACK: And *this* night; was this with her consent?

CHARLES: . . . yes. But. I . . .

JACK: We're listening.

CHARLES: I may have made *promises* to her.

JACK: Do you think her actions abrogate any promises you may have made to her.

CHARLES: No.

JACK: No, you do not.

CHARLES: No.

JACK: Because . . .

CHARLES: I gave her my word.

JACK: I don't understand . . .

CHARLES: I . . .

JACK: You gave her your word to *what*?

CHARLES: I . . .

HENRY: Well, let's get the players straight here, because you want to talk to the *press*, but you don't want to talk to your lawyers.

CHARLES: I gave her my word.

HENRY: That you would do what? What does she *think*, you're going to take her home to *mother*? *(Pause)* That you're going to tell your wife? "Honey, I met this nice *colored* girl."

JACK: . . . huh . . .

HENRY: How'd you meet her? *(Pause)* How'd you meet this girl.

CHARLES: I don't think this is the place.

JACK: How did you meet the girl?

CHARLES: I really do not think this is the place.

JACK: Well, what would be the place? I don't understand.

HENRY: He wants Susan and me to step out.

JACK: He wants you to step out? Why do you say that?

HENRY: Because that's what he wants.

JACK: Is that so?

(Pause.)

CHARLES: Yes.

JACK: *Alright*. Why?

HENRY: Because the girl's a whore.

JACK: Is that it? She's a whore? She's a black whore, and you're upset lest in discussing her you offend a person of her color?

HENRY: Yes.

CHARLES: She isn't a whore.

HENRY: How did you meet her?

CHARLES: I. I would prefer not to tell you.

HENRY: The girl's a whore. He met her through an escort service, or . . .

JACK: You paid the girl? You paid the girl for sex at some time?

CHARLES: I didn't pay her for sex.

JACK: Did you give her money?

CHARLES: Not actually *money*, no I . . .

JACK: What *did* you give her.

CHARLES: I may have, time to time, given her . . .

JACK: You paid her for something.

CHARLES: No. I didn't "pay" her. I . . .

HENRY: What *did* you do?

CHARLES: Well. I bought her *gifts*.

HENRY: You never gave her money?

CHARLES: I *may*. At some *point*. Have lent, or given her *money*. If I "gave her money" does that mean I "paid" her?

JACK: You gave her a "gift"? *(To Henry)* He said he gave her a gift—

CHARLES: Yes. I gave her a gift. An "ongoing . . ."

JACK: An "ongoing gift." Of . . . ?

CHARLES: What *form* it took is no concern . . .

JACK: It doesn't matter to *me* . . .

HENRY: I understand: you gave her a gold watch, or you gave her five thousand dollars a week for . . . ?

CHARLES: That's correct.

HENRY: For *what*?

(Pause.)

CHARLES: If you give your *family* money, is that "paying" them?

HENRY: Yes, it's not quite the same thing.

CHARLES: I . . .

HENRY: Mr. Strickland. Does being black exempt her from the fact that she's a prostitute?

CHARLES: She's not a prostitute.

JACK: What's she do for a living?

HENRY: What's she put on her tax return, Charles? You pull her bank records, lots of cash, checks, fifteen guys, for "consultation" . . .

JACK: The girl's a *whore,* Charles. Irrespective of her race. Or yours. You want to confess, to consorting with a prostitute, do *that,* it's a misdemeanor. *Rape* is a felony. *(Pause)* You feel bad about consorting with a whore don't do it again. That's not what you're *accused* of.

CHARLES: I *exploited* her.

JACK: *Perhaps*. But, *but* you did not *rape* her. *(Pause)* Did you? "Did you *do* it?"

CHARLES: No.

JACK: Well, then. What the *fuck* is this piece of paper? Why do you want to confess?

HENRY: Because he's white.

JACK: Is that a crime?

HENRY: *He* thinks it is.

(Pause.)

JACK: I asked you to, and I'd appreciate it if you *would* . . . Complete for us, if you will, that list of "sins," which is to say, *those things which,* could, at a trial, be used to discredit your testimony. And *get it off your chest.* If you wish to confess to "exploiting" the girl, put it on the list—tell it to the trees. Tell it to God. Do *not* tell it to the press.

HENRY: Tell it to *me*. Tell me what you think you did. Tell it to me.

CHARLES: Alright.

(Henry leads Charles out of the room.)

JACK: I need the report from Kelley. The dress, the material, the *thread,* get me the fucking pattern as we may have to duplicate it.

SUSAN: To duplicate it.

JACK: Here's what I think: if I request the actual dress, the request is, of course, shared with the prosecution. I say we *duplicate* the dress, in all particulars, and restage the supposed assault.

SUSAN: To restage the assault.

JACK: The alleged assault.

SUSAN: Will the judge allow it?

JACK: Cases all day long. Go find them. *(Pause)*

SUSAN: He wants to confess.

JACK: The way to redemption leads through shame. So what? Half any case's in court, other half's dealing with the fucking client.

SUSAN: How do we do that?

JACK: Let Henry do it. He's got more compassion.

SUSAN: You tell the jury she's a prostitute?

JACK: I can't do that.

SUSAN: Why not?

JACK: Why not? Then I'm a white man impugning a black woman's sexuality. You crazy? I got to get this girl out of the picture. Make it a case about a dress. Sex is our weakest card. Now. *Strategically* what do we do? Take the weakest card, and throw it on the table first. We *lead* with it.

SUSAN: Lead with what?

JACK: Sex. You have: to interrupt the thinking process. Of the jury. What is this? I'll tell you what it is, it's a mattress, you know what some people do on it? They *fuck*. And sometimes, they're two different colors. However, *that is not a crime*. *(Pause)* But they may think it is.

SUSAN: Who may?

JACK: *Tell* me.

SUSAN: The jury.

JACK: You're fucking A right. In their mind, it is miscegenation. We've got to walk them *past* it. *We* say, "I know. But watch this: black girl, same size, same dress, white guy, puts her on the bed, and *rolls* on her." Sounds funny? You fucking A bet it is. If you're not doing it, sex looks funny. But it's not a crime.

SUSAN: Unless it is without consent.

JACK: She says that she didn't take her dress off. But, after the demonstration, there's red sequins all over the courtroom. What does that mean? That she *took* her dress off, and she lied. Why did she lie? Because she *understood* that taking the dress off was consent. How do we know? Because she *lied* about it. Why'd she lie? Who cares. Our man goes free.

SUSAN: How did you know I went to Venice?

(Pause.)

JACK: I beg your pardon?

SUSAN: You were speaking of tourism.

JACK: Uh-huh . . .

SUSAN: Of what people remembered. Of their trip. You asked me "what did I remember of my trip to Venice . . ."

JACK: Yes. That's right.

SUSAN: How did you know I went to Venice.

JACK: Everyone goes to Venice.

SUSAN: How did you know *I* went.

JACK: You wrote it on your résumé.

(Pause.)

SUSAN: But it wasn't *on* my résumé.

JACK: I saw it, *I* don't know. Then, I saw it on your, the, I don't know. On your employment application. Foreign travel within the last ten years. You went last year.

SUSAN: It said I went to Rome.

JACK: It said to Rome.

SUSAN: On my employment application.

JACK: Yes, it said "to *Rome*." I beg your pardon.

SUSAN: But you knew I went to Venice.

JACK: Why do you say that?

SUSAN: Because you just confessed it.

JACK: "*Confessed*" it? It was a slip of the tongue.

SUSAN: How is a "slip of the tongue" different from "I misremembered?"

(Pause.)

JACK: I . . .

SUSAN: . . . you *investigated* me.

JACK: *I* don't care why you went to Venice.

SUSAN: That's the wrong answer. You *should* have said, "What do you *mean*?"

JACK: Alright. "What do you mean?"

SUSAN: You investigated me. *(Pause)* Did you? *(Pause)* Before you *hired* me.

JACK: Of course I did.

SUSAN: Why?

JACK: We investigate all new hires.

SUSAN: To that extent?

JACK: To *what* extent?

SUSAN: To the extent of researching their passports?

JACK: Yes.

SUSAN: To that extent.

JACK: Yes.

SUSAN: Are you lying?

JACK: Why would I lie? *(Pause)* Why would I lie?

SUSAN: Why do people lie?

JACK: Well, *you* lied. On your employment form.

SUSAN: Why did *I* lie?

JACK: I don't care. It's not my business.

SUSAN: But you investigated me.

JACK: That's right.

SUSAN: And you found I lied. Then, why would you hire a liar?

JACK: I *presumed* you lied. Because you were, on that trip, involved in let us say, an activity you would not wish to be generally known.

SUSAN: Yes?

JACK: But, which would not impact—any association with the firm.

SUSAN: To wit?

JACK: Oh, come *on* . . .

SUSAN: To wit?

JACK: An Illicit Assignation, a . . . uh . . .

(Pause.)

SUSAN: And you investigate all new hires.

JACK: . . . *please* . . .

SUSAN: Do you?

JACK: Yes. That's correct.

SUSAN: But you felt that the reason for my trip was none of your concern.

JACK: That is correct.

SUSAN: Then why was the question on the form? *(Pause)* Do you investigate all new hires. To the extent to which you investigated me?

JACK: *Susan* . . .

SUSAN: It's a legitimate question. Do you . . .

JACK: I don't know.

SUSAN: Your records show that you do not.

JACK: How would you know that?

SUSAN: I asked Kelley. For the forms.

JACK: Why would he give them to you? Did you use my name?

SUSAN: I didn't use your name.

JACK: Did he assume the request came from me?

SUSAN: How would I know what he assumed?

JACK: Uh-huh.

SUSAN: When I was hired you made the request for an exhaustive background check and a quote complete field investigation.

JACK: Did you allow him to assume the request came from me?

SUSAN: In all your years of operation. You've requested that investigation. Twice. Only twice. *(Pause)* In all the years. *(Pause)* And both applicants were black.

JACK: Is there a difference between causality and correlation?

SUSAN: Both applicants were black. Did you make the "in-depth" request because of their race?

JACK: Susan, sit down.

SUSAN: *Did* you?

JACK: Sit down. I want to tell you something. *Susan*: Sit down. *(Pause)* I. Know. There is nothing. A white person. Can say to a black person. About Race. Which is not both incorrect and offensive. Nothing. I know that. Race. Is the most incendiary topic in our history. And the moment it comes out, you cannot close the lid on that box. That may change. But not for a long long while. *Now, meanwhile,* the laws are such, that I, when I, or, some day, when *you,* even you, employ an African American, should you wish to *discharge* that person, they are armed with the *potential* to allege discrimination. That's a fact.

SUSAN: I . . .

JACK: Which allegation . . .

SUSAN: I . . .

JACK: . . . *which allegation* the courts will most likely accept as proven and the accused stand as guilty until proven innocent.

SUSAN: *"Even* I . . ."

JACK: I, as a judicious businessman, then, *must* investigate. An African-American Applicant with a greater rigor. As I can't ask you *directly,* about your *religion,* about your *family* . . .

SUSAN: I . . .

JACK: To find: "are you a good, moral *person* . . ." I must investigate, to try to *determine* . . .

SUSAN: It's illegal . . .

JACK: . . . your . . .

SUSAN: My qualifications? One would have thought those evident from my résumé.

JACK: No, not your qualifications, your character.

SUSAN: You investigated me, to determine my *"character."*

JACK: That's right.

SUSAN: But you found I had lied. I lied.

JACK: Yes, you lied. But I hired you *anyway,* as I felt the lie (A) was none of my business and (B) was not germane to the determination. What are you bitching about? I gave you a *job.* You want to "change the Racial Tenor of this Country," off you go. *I'm* trying to run a business which supports the *three* of us: fairly and *legally* . . .

SUSAN: It's illegal to apply differing standards of investigation . . .

JACK: Okay, that's illegal. But on the other hand it's *wrong,* you understand? It's "wrong" that folks of different colors are treated differently under the law. It was wrong *then,* and it's wrong *now.* Bullshit *aside*—you are accorded special treatment, I have to take that into account.

SUSAN: You *have* to.

JACK: Yes.

SUSAN: *Why?*

JACK: To run my business.

SUSAN: But it's against the law.

JACK: . . . there you go . . .

SUSAN: Then are you free to break the law?

JACK: You're an Officer of the Court. You lied on your employment application. When you signed it. That's a false admission, with attempt to defraud. Which is a crime.

SUSAN: You were aware of it, and hired me anyway, *which* . . .

JACK: Okay, good for *you*, now: what's the problem? Knock it off.

SUSAN: You hired me anyway.

JACK: Yes.

SUSAN: Why?

JACK: Because you've got talent and it's vastly fucking rare. Now, what do you want from me?

(Pause.)

SUSAN: Why does he want to confess?

JACK: All people want to confess.

SUSAN: White People?

JACK: All people. We have different forms. The whites say "Raise our Taxes," the blacks say, "Fuck you, whitey." Guilt and shame. We Catholics hop into the confessional, the Jews weep on Yom Kippur. I've *seen* 'em. Everyone feels shame.

SUSAN: Blacks feel shame?

JACK: Everyone feels shame.

SUSAN: Is that different from Guilt?

JACK: Guilt is a Legal Term, the "feeling" of guilt, is a sign of our estrangement from God. What's your problem?

SUSAN: You exploited being white.

JACK: Is that what I did?

SUSAN: Yes.

JACK: How?

SUSAN: You investigated me.

JACK: The *firm* investigated you.

SUSAN: That's right.

JACK: So, did *Henry* exploit being white? Or was he just "acting" white, or some such bullshit? In the twenty years we built this firm. And p.s., I'll tell you one more, you tell me that equally, you might not exploit being black? Or that any human being whatever might not, when pressed, exploit whatever momentary advantage he or she possessed. Tell me that, and I'll go give my life to Christ. Just knock it off, and what's the matter, two guys in a room? What is the fucking matter?

(Pause.)

SUSAN: You asked me to wear the dress.

JACK: I asked you to wear the dress.

SUSAN: That's right.

JACK: To wear the Red Dress. *(Pause)* In court.

SUSAN: Yes.

JACK: I'm sorry.

(Pause.)

SUSAN: You're sorry.

JACK: Yes. I was wrong. Will you forgive me? *(Pause)* It's a complicated world. Full of misunderstanding. That's why we have lawyers.

SUSAN: I thought Lawyers existed to seek Justice.

JACK: Well, you were wrong. Two parties to a case—loser ever say, "Yes I lost. But, you know what? The other guy was right." Each side thinks it's right. And *justice*, if it exists—lies only in the imperfect, and mutually unacceptable result of their interaction. What else could it be? I'm sorry I asked you to wear the dress. Will you forgive me?

(Pause.)

SUSAN: Yes, I will.

JACK: Thank you. I very much appreciate it. Now, let's see if we can't settle this thing in our favor.

(Henry enters.)

HENRY: Tell me again.

JACK: Again?

HENRY: Yes. Start from the beginning.

JACK: He said, she said. But the Red Dress was intact.

HENRY: And if our guy's a racist?

JACK: We ain't getting dragged into that pew.

HENRY: What if we are?

JACK: We *aren't*. Full stop. The guy said One Thing, old people next door misheard. Throw it on the table and we're *done* with it.

HENRY: What if there's more?

JACK: Is there more?

HENRY: What if there is.

JACK: Show me.

HENRY: . . . you ready . . . ?

(Henry produces a letter.)

JACK: What is it?

HENRY: Letter messengered to Greenstein.

JACK: Alright.

HENRY: And forwarded to us.

JACK: From whom?

HENRY: A well-wisher.

JACK: Okay . . .

HENRY: Our client's college roommate. A postcard, from our client to his friend. Trip to the Caribbean, college days.

JACK: Read it.

HENRY *(Reads)*: "Bermuda . . ." Our client writes: "Getting off the plane at night. And the heat and the salt air wraps around you." *(Pause)* "It's like being in some hot, black . . ." What is that word? Can you read that word? . . .

(He shows the letter to Jack.)

JACK: Well. That's fucking terrific.

SCENE THREE

The office.
Henry, Jack and Charles.

HENRY *(Showing the postcard to Charles)*: Z'at your handwriting?
CHARLES: What is this?
JACK: Did you write it?
CHARLES: Yes.
HENRY: You *did* write it.
CHARLES: Yes. I wrote it.
HENRY: Alright.
CHARLES: How did you get this?
HENRY: That is your handwriting.
CHARLES: It was, that was *decades* ago, I . . .
HENRY: Who is this "Bill"? Who is "Bill"?
CHARLES: Bill was my roommate.
HENRY: . . . you went to the Caribbean . . .
CHARLES: I . . . we were . . . I was in college. Yes. I wrote him. From the Caribbean.
HENRY: Long time ago.

CHARLES: That's right.

HENRY: Have you had any contact since?

CHARLES: No.

JACK: What you ever do to him?

CHARLES: Do to him? Nothing. We were friends. I wrote to him. From my trip.

JACK *(Reads)*: "Getting off the plane at night. The heat and wet salt air hits you. It's like being in some hot black . . ." *What* is that word?

CHARLES: That's, that's . . . I was speaking. About the *heat* at night. He . . . isn't that *obvious*?

HENRY: Listen to the words. "A hot black cunt."

CHARLES: But, that's not what the words mean.

HENRY: *What's* not what the words mean?

CHARLES: It. It's not a racial epithet.

HENRY: It's *not* a racial epithet . . .

JACK: You want to hear that quote in court?

CHARLES: But it would be taken out of context.

JACK: Well that is the definition of a quote. *(Pause)*

HENRY: Why did he save the letter?

CHARLES: I don't know.

HENRY: That's quite a while ago. Why would he do that?

CHARLES: We save things.

HENRY: Yes, we do.

CHARLES: We . . .

HENRY: We put them in the attic. Yes. We put them in *boxes*.

CHARLES: That's right.

HENRY: And forget them.

CHARLES: Yes.

HENRY: We forget about them.

CHARLES: That's right.

HENRY: But your friend *remembered* this. *(Pause) Why*?

CHARLES: He saw my name in the . . . I don't have to fucking defend myself to you.

HENRY: No, but *we* have to defend *you*. To *defend you*.

CHARLES: He . . .

HENRY: . . . alright.

CHARLES: He saved the letter. Because.

HENRY: Help me through this.

CHARLES: I have a certain . . . a certain *celebrity*.

HENRY: . . . that's good.

CHARLES: Due to my *position*, due . . .

HENRY: Alright.

CHARLES: I . . . he saved the letter because. I am *wealthy* . . . I am . . .

HENRY: Yes.

CHARLES: And when the . . .

HENRY: When the accusation occurred . . .

CHARLES: That's right. *(Pause)* He. *(Pause)* I don't know why he saved the letter.

JACK: You have some "notoriety."

CHARLES: I have, for some time . . .

JACK: But you did *not* in college . . .

CHARLES: Not particularly, no.

JACK: Or for some time afterward.

CHARLES: I . . . No, I . . . Not at all.

HENRY: You fuck some black women while you were down there. In the Caribbean.

CHARLES: Why would he do this to me?

HENRY: What is that?

CHARLES: Why would he save the letter?

HENRY: You can't think of any reason?

CHARLES: No.

HENRY: You fuck some black woman down there?

CHARLES: . . . why would he do this to me?

HENRY: Is he black? *(Pause)* Z'he a black man? This friend.

CHARLES: He's my *friend*.

HENRY: Is he black?

CHARLES: How would you know that from the postcard?

JACK: Is he black?

CHARLES: Yes. *(Pause)* Did you know that from the "list"?

JACK: The list . . . ?

CHARLES: You asked me to write down a list, of my indiscretions . . .

HENRY: . . . and this Bill was your friend.

CHARLES: Yes.

HENRY: As your *friend*, and as a *black* man, how do you think he felt, receiving that postcard?

(Pause.)

CHARLES: We joked about it.

HENRY: You joked about the postcard.

CHARLES: Yes. He found the language "amusing" . . . The language we used . . .

HENRY: You slap palms with him, did you? Back then . . . Talking 'bout the black women in the Caribbean?

JACK: What does he want?

HENRY: I believe he wants reparation.

JACK: How much?

HENRY: I don't think it's money.

JACK: You *don't* think it's money?

CHARLES: You're saying my remark was racist.

(Pause.)

HENRY: You're kidding.

CHARLES: No.

HENRY: The remark on the postcard?

CHARLES: Yes.

HENRY: How can you say that to a black man.

CHARLES: We were friends.

HENRY: Well, then. Let me ask you. Why did he save the letter?

JACK: Why did he save it?

CHARLES: People, people, they "save things."

HENRY: Yes?

CHARLES: They, they keep them in the *attic* . . .

HENRY: As we've *said*, but why did he *remember* it, for all these years?

CHARLES: We *joked* about it. Don't you understand? . . .

HENRY: Yes. But. All these years? . . .

JACK: Hold on, you joked?

CHARLES: We joked about . . .

JACK: Go on.

CHARLES: "Black women . . ."

HENRY *(To self)*: . . . *ah* ha . . .

JACK: What about them?

CHARLES: How . . .

HENRY *(To self)*: . . . *there* it is . . .

JACK: "How?"

CHARLES: How they . . . *(Pause) You* know . . . How they "are more" . . .

JACK: How they are more?

CHARLES: . . . yes . . .

(Pause.)

HENRY: *What?*

(Pause.)

JACK: "Sexually *active*"?

CHARLES: . . . yes.

(Pause.)

HENRY: And are they?

CHARLES: *I* don't know. I . . .

HENRY: But you *joked* about it. That they were more . . . ?

CHARLES: Yes . . .

HENRY: "Promiscuous"?

CHARLES: To my "schoolboy *mind,*" do you understand? I'm not saying it was "right," it *wasn't* right, it was what a young . . .

HENRY: And did your friend share your thoughts?

CHARLES: We *joked* about it.

HENRY: And you talked in a "Negro" voice, and "said" things.

CHARLES: We *both* did.

HENRY: Mister, you've got yourself an enemy.

CHARLES: An "enemy."

HENRY: And how do you think your friend felt? When he thought about that? "Joking" with you. What do you think he felt. Over the years. You're a sensitive man. What did he feel? For "playing along with you"?

CHARLES: Perhaps he felt shame. *(He rises)* Are you done with me?

JACK: Mr. Strickland. With any figure of your prominence. One accusation *will* call forth another. People crave attention, they crave money, "they" are envious and sinful, just like you and me. A case, will grow, and develop, and "declare" itself. As it develops. Just like any illness. Mr. Strickland. All we're talking about is a postcard. Believe it or not, there is nothing here, which will debar us. From winning your case.

CHARLES: . . . I . . . I . . .

JACK: The *fact* remains: that you are *innocent*. And that we can and *will* establish your innocence. In a court of law. Your *innocence. Of that of which you were accused. Irrespective of*: your personal beliefs *or* statements. *Or* prejudices . . .

CHARLES: I believe . . .

JACK: And irrespective *of* whatever *other* true, false, or *arguable* peccadillos or . . .

CHARLES: I believe . . .

JACK: Or sins you may *think* yourself guilty of.

CHARLES: I *believe* . . . that I should talk to the *press*.

JACK: You can't talk to the press.

HENRY: Why would you want to do that?

CHARLES: To explain . . .

JACK: It's our job Mr. Strickland to get you *acquitted*, not to explain. Not to *apologize*. To win the case. Look, everyone wants to be cleansed, it is *attractive* to confess . . . I *understand*, but . . .

CHARLES: . . . I *wronged* that man. I called him my friend. And I did him a great wrong. And I never knew it.

(Susan enters with a sheet of paper.)

JACK: Whatever other "slurs," or acts you may feel yourself accused of. *(Pause)* You've been charged with rape. The charge is unsustainable, and we're going to see that you're exonerated. *(Pause)* You *cannot* confess. You cannot talk to the press. Whatever you feel, *listen* to me. You must *control* your desire to confess. *(Pause; referring to the postcard)* This, *this* man can be bought off.

HENRY: That may not be so, Jack . . .

JACK *(Waving it off)*: Be that as it *may* . . . it has nothing whatever to do with the case at hand.

CHARLES: My friend hated me. I humiliated him. So badly. That he remembered. All these years.

HENRY: Do you know. Mister Strickland.

(Pause.)

CHARLES: What?

HENRY: We all have to put up with a lot. From each other.

(Pause.)

CHARLES *(He starts off)*: That's very generous.

HENRY: I'll walk you out.

(He does so.)

JACK *(To Susan)*: He's been accused of rape. Of which he's innocent. *(Pause)* He hasn't been accused of being racist. *(Pause)* Look, you work in this racket, you are going to meet a lot of people. *At Their Most Human* which is to say "at their worst." There are things *all* of us, would rather . . . *(Susan hands him a sheet of paper)* What is this?

SUSAN: A statement. From the hotel cleaning lady. She now remembers. Finding sequins underneath the bed.

(Pause; she turns to go.)

JACK: Hold the fuck *on*. Tell me again.

SUSAN: They have a statement from the maid who now remembers finding red sequins underneath the bed.

JACK: What prompted her to think again?

(Pause.)

SUSAN: I beg your pardon?

JACK: Why did the cleaning lady think again? She all of a sudden "got the *idea*" . . . ?

SUSAN: I . . .

JACK: . . . to remember something she "forgot"? Why would she *do* that?

SUSAN: How would *I* know?

JACK: How did we get the statement?

(Henry reenters.)

HENRY: . . . what?

JACK *(To Susan)*: Get Kelley on the phone.

(She goes to the phone and dials.)

They've got a statement from the hotel cleaning lady . . . *(He gives it to Henry; to phone)* Hello, *Kelley*. *(Pause)* When? *(Pause)* At whose instigation? *(Pause)* She just "came in"? *(Pause)* The *maid*. *(Pause)* Just "came *in*" . . . You're telling me, some half-literate illegal *hotel* maid, suddenly, takes it upon herself: to go *back* to the police . . .

SUSAN: "Half-literate . . ."

JACK *(Referring to sheet of paper)*: Rosa fucking Gonzales. *(To phone)* I have to call you back.

SUSAN: "Half-literate." Hotel Maid.

JACK: Can we call things: by their name? Her social security number is false, her employment application is written in a misspelled scrawl, she is *illegal*. God *bless* her, that's what she is. *(Pause)* When, in a million *years*, is this woman going *of her own free will* back to the police. In a case, she probably can't even *understand*. To call their attention to a fact that she cannot *possibly* feel is important. *(Pause)* You tell me that. Our client, did our client talk to someone 'cause if not Somebody told the other side, and there's our fucking case, and an innocent man's going to jail. *(Pause)* I do not understand. *(Pause)* Alright . . .

(Pause.)

SUSAN: We . . .

HENRY *(To Susan)*: Susan, I left my briefcase in the car, would . . .
JACK: No. *(To Susan)* She should be here . . . We . . .
HENRY: I need the fucking briefcase.
SUSAN: I'll get it.
HENRY: Thank you.

(She exits.)

JACK: I. Do. Not. Understand. How in the fuckin' *world*. Does this *immigrant*. Suddenly; "get the idea" to remember the sequins. And go to the cops? The fucking cops are "la migra." *(Pause)* The prosecution? Thought of it? They? "Suggested" her? They "planted the idea." I'll take her apart. On the Stand? I'll fucking *murder* her. Okay. We need:
HENRY: . . . the prosecution . . .
JACK: We need her *deposition* . . . Her . . .
HENRY: The prosecution didn't "suggest" her.
JACK: Then where does she suddenly "get the idea"?
HENRY: Did you mind that I sent Susan for the briefcase?
JACK: I don't understand why you need it.
HENRY: I don't need it.
JACK: Then why did you send her away?

(Pause.)

HENRY: Pretty girl.
JACK: Why'd you send her away?
HENRY: Well, I wanted to talk to you alone.

(Pause.)

JACK: Why?
HENRY: Because she sold us out.

(Pause.)

JACK: The *girl* sold us out.
HENRY: That is correct.

JACK: How do you know that? *(Pause)* "Because she's black?"

HENRY: No. Because *I'm* black. And I am not affected, by her bullshit.

JACK: And I am?

HENRY: What the girl has been doing in this office, do you see, Jack, is the postmodern equivalent of a "nigger" act. For the right response, when you ask her to put on the dress, is not, "Fuck you, *whitey*," but, "I'd rather not, and thank you for the job." With a white man you would see that, white woman you *might* see it, black woman, you're blind as a bat.

JACK: Is that so?

HENRY: You bet your life it is.

JACK: And why is that?

HENRY: 'Cause you're guilty?

JACK: What am I guilty about? "Slavery"?

HENRY: No, you weren't here for slavery.

JACK: Then why am I guilty?

HENRY: All people are guilty. Didn't you say that? And she exploited it. And, plus why the fuck *shouldn't* she put on the dress? Is she a member of this firm? I *told* you, Day *One*, not to hire this girl. Day *one*.

JACK: . . . yes you did . . .

HENRY: And you overrode my suggestion.

JACK: You went along with it.

HENRY: I was wrong.

JACK: What *should* you have done?

HENRY: I *should* have told you, "You're a fool."

(Pause.)

JACK: I was *concerned* . . .

HENRY: . . . I'm listening.

JACK: That with her *record* . . .

HENRY: . . . alright.

JACK: With her *credentials* . . .

HENRY: You were concerned she'd sue us. If we turned her down.

JACK: Well, you know what, yes, I *was*.

HENRY: And *now* look what she's done. The girl, do you see, black or white, doesn't make a difference, she's *trouble* . . .

JACK: And you knew that on Day One.

HENRY: Her *thesis*, Jack, in *college*. Her college thesis was on . . . *(Takes a paper and reads)* "Structural Survivals of Racism in Supposedly Bias-free Transactions." Quote. "The nexus of oppression is ineluctable. Even the consciousness of the oppressor, indeed, this consciousness least of all, is capable of expunging from his acts and utterances the dialectic of dominance." *(Pause)* You think, Jacky, you are immune. Because you understand the problem. What you don't see, is, that, to her, you *are* the problem. And you're so fucking proud of yourself. For not making a pass at her, for "respecting" her as a "human being," that you do *not* see, this ungrateful little girl, looking at me, and, in her eyes, "where is your *watermelon*." While her privileged, Affirmative Action self is here on a pass, Jack, on a motherfucking pass. Which you gave her. *However* smart she is. *(Pause)* I would be mortified, to go through life, thinking that I'd received a dispensation because of my race. And I am ashamed of her that she is not. *(Pause)* And she sold us out. Because of the Race of our client. Who is innocent. *(Pause)* That's all.

JACK: "She sold us out"?

HENRY: She called the prosecution with the information on the dress, and I'll bet you a *fucking dollar*, that she called the college roommate.

JACK: How would she get his name?

HENRY *(Holds up a piece of paper)*: . . . whose name appears on the "List of Sins" you had him write. *(Reads)* "I used to go 'tomcatting' with my college friend, Bill . . ."

(Susan reenters with the briefcase.)

Susan, may I ask you something?

SUSAN: Of course.

HENRY: When our client came in, did you ask him for a check?

SUSAN: That's right.

HENRY: Why?

SUSAN: You told me to keep him occupied.

JACK *(Simultaneous with "occupied")*: But, we've had several clients before, whom you spoke to. Did you do that with them? *(Pause)* Did you?

SUSAN: I was doing as I was asked.

JACK: But you never did it before.

SUSAN: I don't understand where you're going.

HENRY: And you called the Court—to have us listed as Attorneys of Record.

SUSAN: That's not why I called the court.

HENRY: Why did you call the Court?

SUSAN: Kelley was unavail . . . Why do you *think* I called the court?

HENRY: Perhaps you *wanted* the client here.

SUSAN: Of course I wanted him here. I believed *you* wanted him here.

HENRY: Well—we were in the process of deciding when your act committed us. You believe he's guilty.

SUSAN: I think it's irrelevant.

JACK: But you believe he's guilty.

SUSAN: In fact I do.

JACK: You believe he is.

SUSAN: I'm certain of it.

JACK: When did you reach that conclusion?

(Pause.)

SUSAN: I, I don't know. I *read,* in his . . . you asked him to write a, to write a *confession*, of the things he'd done, I . . .

HENRY *(To Jack)*: . . . you *see*?

JACK *(To Susan)*: You said you thought he was guilty when you first saw him. Because I asked you what you thought. And you told me that he "looked" guilty. *(Pause)* But you say now, You always *knew* he was guilty.

SUSAN: The evidence seems to indicate he is.

JACK: Yes, but you thought so previous to the evidence. *(Pause)* You thought so when you first *saw* him.

SUSAN: That's right.

JACK: Why?

(Pause.)

SUSAN: We all have prejudices.
JACK: Yes, that's right.
SUSAN: But we try to *suspend* them.
JACK: We do?
SUSAN: In the interests of our client.
JACK: And what were *your* prejudices?
SUSAN: Women are taught. *(Pause)* To be wary of men.
JACK: Anything else?

(Pause.)

SUSAN: He's *white.*
HENRY: Thank you and is a white man entitled to legal representation?
JACK: . . . and so you were *doubly* prejudiced against him.
SUSAN: That's right.
JACK: Because he was white.
SUSAN: White men have traditionally exploited black women.
JACK: And is that prejudice?
SUSAN: Perhaps it is. And perhaps I was conscious of it. And strove to put it aside.
JACK: But you thought he was guilty.
SUSAN: No. I was sure he was guilty.
JACK: And did you think he should be punished?

(Pause.)

SUSAN: I thought he *would* be punished.
JACK: You thought he *should* be punished.
SUSAN: That is correct.
JACK: By *you*?
SUSAN: Not by me, no.
JACK: By whom?
SUSAN: By the court.

JACK: That's the wrong answer. The *right* answer is, "What are you getting at?" *(Pause)* . . . that's the wrong answer . . .

HENRY: Did you sell us out?

SUSAN: When did you cease to trust me?

HENRY: Did you sell us out?

SUSAN: Did you trust me, when you hired me?

HENRY: Jack did. I didn't.

SUSAN: Why?

HENRY: Because you lied. On your employment form.

SUSAN: *Uh*-huh.

HENRY: D'you call the prosecution? You call the roommate? Susan?

SUSAN: . . . but your partner, took a chance on me.

HENRY: That's right.

SUSAN: Why? *(Pause. To Jack)* Why?

JACK: How the fuck do *I* know? Because you came up the hard way. 'Cause you're smart, 'cause you're black, 'cause you're young and pretty. Is it all a *crime* now? Is it all a crime?

SUSAN: You mistrust me, because I'm black.

JACK: Say I *do*. Did I have reason to?

SUSAN: Did you?

JACK: You lied on your employment form.

SUSAN: Is that something "black" people do?

JACK: Uh-huh.

SUSAN: If you mistrusted me why in the world did you *hire* me?

JACK: I mistrusted you but I *suppressed* it.

SUSAN: Why?

JACK: Because you are black . . .

SUSAN: . . . because I'm black . . .

JACK: . . . and I thought. I *thought* you deserved a *chance. Alright?* And I gave you a chance and you betrayed me.

SUSAN: On what evidence?

HENRY: *Deny* it . . .

JACK: Just deny it Susan. *(Pause)* Tell me I'm wrong. *(Pause)* The man's innocent.

SUSAN: *Is* he? . . .

JACK: "*Is* he?" What the fuck does *that* mean? The man's our *client*. He's our *client* . . .

(The phone rings. Henry answers the phone.)

HENRY *(To phone)*: Yes, go ahead.

JACK: And an innocent man is going to have his life ruined. By *you*. You sold us out. You sold our *client* out. Didn't you?

SUSAN: "An innocent man."

JACK: Get out of my sight. Get out of my sight, you fucking ingrate.

(She rises to go.)

SUSAN: You forgot to say "nigger."

JACK: Get out of my sight.

HENRY *(To phone)*: Yes. *(Pause)* Thank you. *(He hangs up; to Jack)* That was the District Attorney. *(Pause)* The rookie, first responding officer. *(Pause)* Has just discovered and submitted, a page of his initial report. In which he describes the room "covered in sequins." He left it in the pocket of his coat. *(Pause)* And our client. Has just confessed. To the rape.

JACK: Susan . . .

SUSAN: Do you want me to tell you about White People? *(Pause)* The silver spoon was missing and you fired the maid. *(Pause)* You cannot help yourselves. And you wonder how black people feel about you? As you said. We know. You will betray us. Every chance you get. Like children. Like sick children. *(To Henry)* Didn't this fool know that man raped that girl? *(Pause)* Didn't *you* know? . . . *You* knew—didn't you *care*? . . .

(She starts to exit.)

HENRY: You didn't send the information on the dress.

SUSAN: I've told you I did not.

HENRY: But you called the college roommate.

SUSAN: I don't know what you mean . . .

(She shrugs and begins gathering her things to exit.)

HENRY: 'Cause, we can tell them, that man remembered that "slight" over thirty years. But you and I know it's untrue.

SUSAN: Is it untrue?

HENRY: Man of that age? Shit he's had to eat? That fucking "slight" was *nothing* to him.

SUSAN: It was his college roommate.

HENRY: It was some *white* boy who he knew in college. He didn't even remember till you called him up. *You* called the roommate up. You ginned him up. *Didn't* you?

SUSAN: Is that what I did?

HENRY: And your act. Was a violation of the law.

SUSAN: As was yours, when you had me investigated.

JACK: Did you betray me?

SUSAN: In any event it would have had no bearing on the justice of the case.

JACK: You tell me why.

SUSAN: Because, White Man, he was guilty.

END OF PLAY

BRIGITTE LACOMBE

DAVID MAMET is the author of many plays, including *Glengarry Glen Ross* (Pulitzer Prize, 1984), *American Buffalo, The Cryptogram, A Life in the Theatre, November, Boston Marriage* and *The Woods*.